mycelium.

debora Ewing

'was once' was published May 2020, and 'my real face' and 'rankled' published January 2021 by Dodging the Rain https://dodgingtherain.wordpress.com/

'paper boats' was published October 2020 and 'clock-hours' February 2021 by Loose Words https://medium.com/loose-words

'watershed' audio version was published by Iambic Beats https://iambicbeats.bandcamp.com/

Cover Art: *Mycelium* by debora Ewing, acrylic on canvas
Book Design by Shannon Mastromonico

I am indebted to my entangled poetesses: melons, blue, lise, and shan – you're all my fifth stickers;

to Heather, always, for the things we know;

to my poet-guru, Peter Kidd, and to his love/my coach, Linda Stone – they each and both guided me through many states;

to Rob Haight, who taught me the things I didn't think I wanted to know about poetry, even how to write acknowledgements;

and

with love to Mom, who always believes in me.

mycelium.

1. tuesday morning rain clouds
2. functional love
3. weekends
4. mycelium
5. meltdown
6. terra cotta
7. watershed
8. unwritten
9. was once
10. cassandra
11. baleadas
12. rankled
13. tempest
14. my real face
15. timing
16. the next show starts in ten minutes
17. paper boats
18. recoil
19. melancholia
20. lacuna
21. fireflies
22. ocotillo tongue
23. solstice
24. water peace
25. für Lise
26. legends
27. hallows
28. song to my many loves
29. screen time
30. equinox
31. separado
32. clock-hours
33. the burning
34. coffee grounds
35. diablera

tuesday morning rain clouds

early thunder with coffee
raindrops splashing my cup
boots
hair
pathways across
my face like tears
of God's love
Here is my church.

last bat races the sky
dips under whispering
budded branches

two foxes jump and play
in the rain
with abandon
under the biggest Norway spruce

words half-spoken
dreams fading
magnolias open
remembrance

thunder gives way to tires
splattering potholes leaving
exhaust in the wake

the sound of full drops plopping
on old leaves is pure grace
I pour my second cup
but
take these self-imposed tenets
back to bed instead
and have a second waking

I almost let go once

1

functional love

I fell in love with you in a dream
you asked me to park your other truck
I was hung up on explanation
logistics
maybe geometry
I handed over the keys

as you took the metal chain
you held my finger lost in thought
I crooked it a little
complicit
waiting
and like that
the thing was done

dreams release
the same dopamine as life
withdrawal is quicker come morning
a cold slap before coffee

you held my finger
I crooked it a little
like that the thing
was done

and then I awoke
and now I am lost

weekends

respite isn't itself
as workday recedes
leaving a dry wadi
bare
smooth
taupe

creatures creep forth into this meek bed
howl shadows of a promise so strong
as to eclipse mountains

rustle my pillow with scratchy-paws
whisper love lost in old grains of sand

were sentiments like pennies
they could accrue with each drop into the jar
eventually weighing enough
to influence the universe

but that's not how it works, love
feelings are processes
writhing, volatile
conduits
mind to heart

best to remember
there's a gateway
at each end

mycelium

which is heavier
longing
or
acceptance

when the sun's rays press you down
into leaves and cobblestones

blackbirds laugh
squirrels rifle the forest bed
and
mycelium
is wary to wake

maybe

one
single
feather
sifted
through
winter's sigh

is enough
to lighten the load

meltdown

this blue-green fat beetle
I worship like a totem
spiracle-breath on my finger
yet I contemplate

his shell under my foot
crunched into the gravel
whether I'd survive whole
the devastation
of killing him

terra cotta

lost in my own sun war
I spit with distaste at the cold circumference
cumulus-circles like carrion eaters
whine in the shadows

I should not be here

sparrows retreat to the north
and the crows judge from treetops
dropping crystalline epithets
in my path

I am dying of love

like a plant with roots
too big for its canopy
suffocating under my own well-wishes
crying penny-drops unrequited

we will refuse each other

watershed

rain comes gently
at first - I know
by some route
it came from you
this is how we touch

I don't know your name
but I know your taste
how this rain traced
your shape as it fell
light on wet streets

rain seals the death of us
in leaves of last autumn
pressed into beetles
something permanent
some quiet rumble

harder now
tapping like fingers
insistent these drops
that in another season
would be snow

take me by
way of my DNA
out to the watershed
to the sound to the sea
salted into clouds
to fall again
to you

unwritten

I cling stubbornly to this unlovable love
swirl in my soul like stirred coffee
creamy, bitter, warm
the satisfaction is temporary

easily digested, refill and repeat

the math doesn't support the daydream
we're leaves swirling on eddies
poured out under gutters filled
by an indifferent monsoon

how should I reconcile reality with ideal
and which one is which?

meantime I curl like a cat
keep comfortable the empty space
for real love to incubate

eventually

was once

this thing I called love
once wild once cumbersome
I'm learning to hold
keep it calm and warm
distract it with stories and
shiny things sometimes
lull it to sleep
let it tap gently on my face
in the early hours waking

this thing was once
our downfall misunderstanding
a result of being handed wrong
sets of expectation like
faulty algebra or
an instruction manual
for someone else's machine
no wonder
it didn't work right

this softness
I don't scream at it don't
press it down into my bowels
where it can do the most damage
this thing I called love once
sits with me sometimes
climbs over my shoulders
tangles my hair
whispers its true name
too quietly to hear

we don't call it that word
anymore

cassandra

crow-chatter tinkles
like sundrops on the garden
I am calm in the face of maybe

yes I've weathered storms
like the one I think is coming
the crows are not alarmed

aesthetic in pocket
statistics say I'm no match
a non sequitur

let the day come and go
like the entropy of breathing
light rain in the yard after

baleadas

biding time
in a Latin café
baleadas y tamarindo
the latest pop videos

at the same time
a better construct of Me
is 3K miles away
warm in your pocket
sharing coffee
and biscuits
and kisses

besitos y conchas
y tu tambien

en mi bolsillo
tambien

rankled

the world is full of bad math
the truth of me is
unequal to lessons
bound in prophetic pages
writ in ancestors' blood
all we decry as holy
or
holier-than-me

a blister on the belly of a moth
holds more truth than this

tempest

this rain is not angry enough
petting my forehead
a caress of *calm down*
here's a glass of water

no

I am a tempest
screaming raw pebbles at the road
in my own defense hurling
soft words into the treetops

and they shy knowing
betrayal is a swifter punishment
than being misunderstood
can I really be so fragile

one feather will knock me over
just a question mark sends my head
spinning in the other direction
I struggle to find the thread
before you ask me again

so it's habit then
closing everybody's tickets
shut off inquiry like
a drainpipe and there's
that feather
fallen

the rain comes harder now
as if to say it understands
another layer
between
us

my real face

        mania clears
     and I sweep up the shards
      dreams not ill-pursued
         but stunted
  life cycles will be what they will

all those times I almost didn't go
I hold them lovingly
pillbug-curled
would have been easier

      I make my own coffee again
          look - I've been cut
         again

this hematopoietic slow kiss
reminds me I am still real
not a singularity

     and I rise to the call of crows

timing

the still-birth
of our friendship
hurts me no less

than had bloom truly blossomed
had ants crawled over bud
coaxing it open
letting us bee-sleep within

and then faded in its due season
dropped withered petals
to the snow

I have few regrets
but this picture
of your kiss

the next show starts in ten minutes

I'm resentful of words
and their clever implications
poised on the ball
of one foot, hands clasped
behind the back
ear turned up small-smiled
waiting
for nods and applause
when

the real story
leans against a wall
greasy-haired
twirls an unlit cig
chokes a laugh
at tonight's irony

paper boats

precepts have fallen
spiral like errant feathers
dipping gently into rainbow
rippled oil-slick puddles
where the asphalt sank
and everyone who said it matters
doesn't even
see
I'm floating away

bereft of syllables
I push grass and gravel back
into my foxhole
that emptiness too familiar
I don't want it
I return

to my poorly-filled den
seep gasoline between
silt and root
and
set it on fire

recoil

I close my eyes and feel torsion on my soul
to languish in the desert would be
better than this

or would it
would that gritty furnace mitigate enthalpy
or would I explode
fault-line-shaking

my fabric is permeable
and I ease between molecules
multiversed in space-time
untethered
homeless

let me dissipate into arroyo sand
let these sentiments I leak
contract without sun
and fall stomachward
like stars
in the palm
of God's hand

nothing is linear
                not really

melancholia

these misty days
a bit warmer we'd call them sultry
are best for musing

with tea with honey
the purpose of butter knives
late-night dorm windows
dismal Caribbean alleys
industrial evolution
horsehair to armchair
the nonlinear become commonplace

this crow outside
picks a ladybug off the window
his feet not touching the ground
now there's a balancing act
I wonder if he knows

lacuna

ay, lacuna
gift of possibilities
hidden, extant
I drink you with
my tears

lacuna full
of all these things:
sands and wheelbarrows
lithops & gumbos
wrenches, weeds, teacups
sad chacarera
Halloweens

if every star could fall
across my face
weave a path
like salt
yes

I might be more alive
but I see you
lacuna
reminding me

I'm here
against
the crescent

fireflies

everything's so fleeting
these violets
this rain

this bitterness
this joy
this tedium
this gratitude
these expectations

just under the surface
topsoil and pain are constant
regret is a choice

like planting pumpkins
enough for the deer
and children, too

fireflies are only
a season

ocotillo tongue

scratch my skin
with your ocotillo tongue
the desert drinks my blood
and a year's worth of tears

this arroyo blooms for us
only for a week or so
don't be gentle on me, love
bring the sand, bring the storm

worry not about my bones
let the beetles pick them clean
until next spring

water peace

the sound you make
gentle patter against leaves
rolling over smooth veins
shaking loose peat fragrance between roots
of irritated but also thirstful grass
quiet scratchings of slipper claws
against damp skin

how I imagine
contentment

standing amid your poetry
love-words tangle pathways
in my hair
bind it to my skin
whisper down my nape
if

we stay here long enough between
susurrus and tree-throat promises
you'd take me down
with you

into the deepest
silent aquifers

and twilight, and forgetting.

Solstice

I found myself
for today
in this old sweater
leather boots
the right lipstick
carnelian necklace
you're a ghost to me

and you don't know
I'm wasting
rusty red flesh
among auburn leaves
where the trees
speak your promise
but not
your
name

Für Lise

this ripe field is not enough for us, love
each rye spike sheds its name in our footprints
brash clouds race your laughter
pulling trees over the horizon yet

this city is not enough for us either
the buildings can claw no higher
and birds drop mockery
where our grandfathers drafted
pale dreams in varied blue but

we need a bed as wide as our minds
full with linen pages and ink spilled over
into the next morning with
lazy feathers and coffee
falling half-truths
into our mouths

we've earned this much

legends

they'll tell our stories later
wild glory but not the laundry
dramatic poses but not putting away dishes
recycling on curb-side
deciding what to wear today
or eat

they'll name us well
but our tired bones they'll nudge
one-footed cornerwise
our true names only
web-woven
by spiders

hallows

in the dank silence of the weekend
you come to me like floodwaters

fevered kisses steaming
Ford pickup windows shattered
bottles against basement walls
steroid crash nausea that
ring you bought me
from our daughter
for a dollar

the way you never told me
you weren't coming with me

your memory falls on my face like cold
autumn rain your apology falls bitter
a wind blowing dark leaves
across your grave

I know, my love
I'm sorry too

song to my many loves

send me four kisses and the joy of being a parent
memories of talks behind laundry carts
ale and distasteful composition

give me three rocks from under the house
two pages of Shakespeare and a kiss
left between shoulder blades

take back your ticket to Chicago
mother's chiding and her empty promises
the lifetimes before we met

bring me unadorned truth and a question
on a small piece of paper in the parking-lot
six-pack in the living-room

and you, the one that can't be written
please keep it all
and the moon just less than full

I let you go every day
    a thousand times every day

screen time

one day I may count
the poems I've written you
more than twenty-three
last I knew

my private jokes on unlined paper
fond memories of lives
never to pass
and yet

somewhere
according to inexact
laws of space-time
they're still rolling

like a projector
the operator's

long since

abandoned

29

Separado

a mountain on the horizon
        drawn in tea leaves

                a fleeting equation in old math

sad ranchero tuba-plaints
                        your eyes
voicing what an arroyo cannot speak
through the cotton of your mouth

                the skeleton of your hand drawing my lungs
                        rising toward the east, falling
                            into murmuration
                                    bitter snow

equinox

I fell out of words
there are no bats this morning
no absence of reason
just a heavy mist
and commuters and eggs
and
a second chance

the sun rises pumpkin-fire on the forest edge
still the moon through a lacy veil
big juicy wedge smiling
into my coffee

oh yes this is why I've come
I try to stay until I'm calm

I turn toward the red door
my belly warm with oil and maple
the trees beg me to stay

just a little longer
hear: we're clasping tight
our leaves for you

and I do
I hear, and I stay
a little longer

clock-hours

some days it occurs to me
how many poems have been lost
in how many lifetimes
ill-conceived plots
wild passes
dreams that looked so very real

words dash off the nib onto paper
and the paper falls to floor
trod upon in the tumult
of staying afloat

priorities can spin on a pinhead

suddenly I realise
all my words already have been written
giving them that much less impact
this page feels like such a waste

but words self-seed
come back in another season taller
more vigorous branches
facing the new sun

there's always next year

the burning

how can I show you utter magic?
a sound of rain on last year's autumn
over the dull roar of highway and
orange city lights rumbled against the cloud

how can I encapsulate
dragon's blood on wedding cedar
drunken blue pea, desert sage, wormwood
love-words from Africa

how can I convey this wind
as it stops short of my circle
curls around the fire, lies at my feet
trees humming in ancient songs and
rocks almost indiscernibly
dancing

hold your hand up to the sky
feel my touch, my love
it's our magic

coffee grounds

the prophecies in my mug are always mountains
and it's time I acknowledge
the medium may influence the outcome

unless
these mountains are allegory
the figures not you
not me
well, obviously

one of them has to be me
but maybe not figures

I liked the one with the goat
I wish more prophecies
were silly like that

best pour another cup of sanity
and get back to data
manipulation

diablera

I've been asleep
torturous battles in my dreams
emerged ragged
not quite victorious
boot-dragging across the brick

the café was repainted
while I was out
scrubbed with hard brushes
tattered shutters resplendent
like fresh wings for the
coming storm
un café más, Señora

and I, too, will paint myself
war-drum colors
plátano gold
snapper-tooth sharp
agua de jamaica loud
from one to the other coast

I'm almost done
whittling my pencils
let's do this

notes

www.ingramcontent.com/pod-product-compliance
Lightning Source LLC
Chambersburg PA
CBHW060544030426
42337CB00021B/4422